S0-ABD-988

USING COMPUTER SCIENCE IN
HOSPITALITY
≫ CAREERS ≪

JENNIFER CULP

Rosen
YA™
New York

Published in 2020 by The Rosen Publishing Group, Inc.
29 East 21st Street, New York, NY 10010

Copyright © 2020 by The Rosen Publishing Group, Inc.

First Edition

Library of Congress Cataloging-in-Publication Data

Names: Culp, Jennifer, 1985– author.
Title: Using computer science in hospitality careers / Jennifer Culp.
Description: First edition. | New York, NY : The Rosen Publishing Group, Inc., 2020. | Series: Coding Your Passion | Includes bibliographical references and index. | Audience: Grades 7 to 12.
Identifiers: LCCN 2018044838 | ISBN 9781508187165 (library bound) | ISBN 9781508187158 (pbk.)
Subjects: LCSH: Hospitality industry—Vocational guidance—Juvenile literature. | Hospitality industry—Data processing—Juvenile literature.
Classification: LCC TX911.3.V62 C85 2020 | DDC 647.94023—dc23
LC record available at https://lccn.loc.gov/2018044838

Manufactured in China

CONTENTS

INTRODUCTION

Hospitality is a huge umbrella industry encompassing a wide variety of careers in guest lodging, event planning, and transportation. This resource explores the intersection between technology and hospitality, revealing the ways in which computers and digital technology drive and expand the field of guest services. In a world revolutionized by technologies such as app-enabled ride- and home-sharing services, hospitality combines high-tech innovation with human expertise and charm to offer the best possible guest experience in the modern world.

Technology is woven into the very fabric of the hospitality industry. Digital systems make all aspects of booking and managing lodging not only possible but also increasingly convenient for both travelers and hotel workers. Apps allow customers to search for, book, check into, and review hospitality businesses. Social media has expanded the reach of conventional advertising, allowing visitors to high-end hotels to show off photos of their surroundings. Tech adoption has also allowed smaller, nontraditional lodging businesses to flourish, offering luxury experiences at affordable prices.

The constant innovation and use of ever-more sophisticated digital programs and devices affects every individual involved in the hospitality industry, shaping the experiences of every traveler and

Technology informs every aspect of lodging, travel, and food-service businesses, but ultimately the hospitality industry operates on face-to-face human interaction.

employee. Hospitality employees throughout the industry utilize new technologies to carry out their work. Concierges and front desk staff use point of sale and property management system software programs to take payments and check guests in and out of rooms, ensuring that the hotel is never overbooked, while valets use similar programs to keep track of guests' vehicles.

Automated room temperature sensors and automatic light shutoff save energy for the hotel and simplify housekeeping's responsibilities. Global positioning system devices with alert buttons help protect housekeeping employees and other hotel workers from potentially dangerous encounters with guests. And finally, hotels employ a number of maintenance workers who are responsible for keeping the hotels' tech itself functioning optimally.

Furthermore, the continual implementation of new tech in hospitality provides opportunities for digital innovators who create the programs and devices that streamline travel and lodging experiences. Software developers are needed to create and maintain internet-based and mobile applications that allow guests to book hotel rooms, summon rides, and leave reviews and ratings.

Embedded software developers who create "smart" devices, such as virtual assistants and responsive touchscreen appliances, revolutionize the look and feel of traditional hotel rooms. These technologies connect everyday objects such as mirrors and clocks to the internet to provide guests with convenient and comfortable access to services. Web developers build attractive websites to intrigue customers and secure bookings.

It takes a village to provide twenty-first-century hospitality experiences for travelers, and nearly every aspect of the industry is associated with technology in some way.

CHAPTER ONE

THE EVOLUTION OF HOSPITALITY CAREERS

It takes a talented team of people to keep a hotel running smoothly at all times. There are many different jobs available under the hospitality umbrella, all of which require different skill sets and all of whom interact with technology in different ways.

When you first think of walking into a hotel, you might think of the concierge, who helps answer questions and resolve problems; the front desk staff, who greet and check in guests; the bellhops, who transport luggage to and from rooms and provide transportation to and from the hotel; or the valets, who park and retrieve guests' cars.

However, even more people work behind the scenes to ensure that hotel guests enjoy a relaxing experience. Housekeeping workers, engineering and facilities maintenance, administrative staff, human resources officers, guest services operations employees, and even security are categorized by

Tech in lodging businesses goes beyond the computers at the front desk. Specialized programs aid workers in organizing guests, parking, and even laundry services.

Marriott as the Quality Keepers. They are the driven, detail-oriented staffers who work to provide both guests and fellow employees with a safe, pleasant experience at the hotel.

THE BACKBONE OF HOSPITALITY

Housekeeping makes sure every room stays clean and sanitary, operates cleaning machinery, and keeps an eye on in-room appliances to make sure everything works properly. Tech maintenance staff ensures that the facilities operate at peak performance, fixing any problems that may arise with electricity, plumbing, and structural issues with the building; managing the vehicle fleet; and communicating with one another throughout the day and overnight to coordinate activities.

At Hyatt hotels, engineering staff maintains responsibility for the overall maintenance of the premises, requiring expertise in building and repairing heating, air conditioning, and electrical systems, plus large kitchen and laundry equipment. Dedicated employees in this sector could potentially progress through a career path from general maintenance handyperson, to specialty technician, to shift manager, or even head of engineering. Administrative staff uses digital systems to manage the hotel's daily business and handle the business's financial and practical concerns, while human resources staff provides oversight and advocacy for everyone who works under the hotel's umbrella, hiring and training new employees to fill various roles within the organization.

Financial experts maintain budgets and expenditure forecasts, perform audits, and oversee monthly income statements. At Hyatt hotels, finance-focused employees can expect to progress from account clerk to staff accountant to credit manager, potentially even supervising the department as director of finance.

Security officers use high-tech digital and electronic systems to communicate with one another and other hotel staff, monitor vulnerable areas, and prevent illicit

Happy hotel staff, such as a concierge, a specialized employee who assists guests by making recommendations and reservations for food, travel, and entertainment, bring expertise to hospitality.

activity on the premises, using intricate alarm systems that alert appropriate authorities in the case of any criminal behavior on the property.

All of these different jobs require oversight and management themselves, depending on the leadership positions Marriott refers to as the Planners. General and departmental managers coordinate hotel employees' efforts. Operations managers, directors of finance, directors of banquets, sales and marketing teams, and restaurant managers are a few of the other jobs Marriott lists as essential to operations on its careers website.

WORKING WITH HOSPITALITY TECH

Other positions in hospitality are directly tied to technical proficiency. Information technology managers oversee the digital concerns of a hotel or rental business, installing, removing, and troubleshooting the business's hardware and software, perhaps even assisting in making purchasing decisions related to new technology.

Computer systems analysts are also found in hotel environments, working to set up, operate, and maintain tech functionality; ensuring internet connectivity and proper data management; maintaining local networks; and providing information technology support services to guests and staff as needed.

Network security analysts are required to detect and deter cyberthreats. These experts must continually work to remain aware of emerging trends in cybercrime and understand how best to prevent it from affecting a hotel's networks and guests. Tech security professionals may even perform penetration tests on a hotel's networks themselves, essentially attempting to hack sensitive systems in order to determine where they may be vulnerable and require protection.

These jobs require extensive education in computer science. Most job openings of this sort ask that candidates hold at least a four-year bachelor's degree in computer science, engineering, or a related field to ensure that tech-focused employees begin their work with the necessary expertise to fulfill their responsibilities and maintain the organization's efficiency and safety. Experience in hospitality is also preferred, so a candidate who has both the necessary technical education and experience working in another area of hospitality, such as front desk support, may be preferred to a tech expert who has no background in guest services.

HOSPITALITY HOMEWORK

Many full-service hotel chains prefer to hire candidates who hold a bachelor's degree in hospitality or hotel management, which provides students with training in hotel administration, accounting, marketing and sales, housekeeping, food service management and catering, and even hotel maintenance and engineering.

Systems training in various digital programs and products is an important part of a hospitality bachelor's program, notes the *Occupational Outlook Handbook*, as hotels use industry-specific software to manage reservations, billing, housekeeping schedules, and other concerns throughout the course of the day-to-day business. Licenses and professional certifications are not necessarily required to secure employment in the industry, but some exist and may be helpful when it comes to securing a job.

High school students are eligible to participate in the Hospitality and Tourism Management Program, a two-year training program that prepares young people for future hospitality management careers. Offered by the American Hotel & Lodging Educational Institute, completion of the program leads to a professional certification. College students and working professionals can seek recognition by American Hotel & Lodging Educational Institute and STR, Inc., a US company that tracks global hospitality industry data, by completing the Certification in Hotel Industry Analytics examination. This exam tests candidates' knowledge of hotel industry practices, math fundamentals, data comparison between properties, and industry-wide performance reports.

EMPLOYEE SAFETY THROUGH TECH

In addition to providing convenience, technology helps to ensure safety and protect hospitality employees. A survey of five hundred female hospitality workers in the Chicago area by the industry union Unite Here revealed that 58 percent of female hotel employees and 77 percent of female casino workers had been subjected to sexual harassment by guests, and a 2017 analysis by the Center for American Progress found that more than 14 percent of sexual harassment complaints filed with the US Equal Employment Opportunity Commission between

Security systems help protect both guests and workers at lodging businesses. Security staff communicate with one another and prevent dangerous scenarios from unfolding.

2005 and 2015 came from the hotel and restaurant industry, making up the highest percentage of such reports from any industry on record.

Major hotel chains such as Marriott International Inc. and Hilton Worldwide Holdings Inc. have been investing in high-tech solutions to ensure workers' and guests' safety, pledging to equip employees who enter guests' rooms with panic-button devices that use global positioning satellite technology to alert management and security if an employee finds himself or herself or a guest in a dangerous or threatening situation. Marriott and Hilton intend to supply all employees in their US hotels with the safety devices by 2020, and InterContinental Hotels Group and Wyndham Hotels & Resorts Inc. are working to develop guidelines for appropriate threat response for franchise owners.

Hyatt Hotels Corporation has already adopted the devices in 120 of its hotels in both North and South America and plans to standardize their inclusion across all the company's managed and franchised hotels. According to STR Inc., a research company that tracks hotel industry data, brands owned by Marriott, Hilton, InterContinental, Wyndham, and Hyatt account for 45 percent of all the hotel rooms in the United States, and their commitment to backing safety with technology is expected to improve working conditions for potentially vulnerable hotel workers.

In Washington, DC; Seattle, Washington; Chicago, Illinois; Las Vegas, Nevada; and Miami Beach, Florida, hospitality workers' unions have successfully lobbied to make panic button devices mandatory in hotels, and unionized hospitality workers in New York City have been equipped with the devices since 2012. "Protecting our employees and the millions of guests who stay in our hotels each day is of paramount importance to the industry," said Katherine Lugar, president and chief executive of the American Hotel and Lodging Association in a *New York Times* article.

EMPLOYEE SATISFACTION

The comfort of guests is the backbone of the hotel and lodging field, but employee satisfaction makes this happen. Turnover in the hospitality industry (including travel and food) tends to be high in comparison to many careers.

The frustration leading to such high rates of burnout may be at least in part due to poor adoption of technology and too much work as a result of understaffing. To fix these problems, several things come into play. First, businesses that embrace technological innovation should have adequate amounts of staff, rather than attempt to replace jobs with automation. For example, according to the creators of Connie, Hilton hotels' robot concierge, the device is intended not only to provide information to guests but also to improve the staff experience by freeing them to deal with complex concerns instead of spending time on basic questions from guests. Connie isn't meant to be a full-stop replacement for human management and concierges.

The adoption of new technologies in hospitality serves to increase both employee and guest satisfaction, streamlining processes and making everyone's experiences more pleasant.

The staff experience should be considered at the start of adopting new technology. Both guests and staff benefit from simple, easy-to-use innovations that don't require a lot of training, wrote Uli Pillau, CEO of the property management system provider Apaleo, in an article for Hospitality.net. Insufficient training time and investment may lead to confusion and frustration, particularly in an understaffed establishment. "Usability is paramount, especially for core technologies, when turnover rates are high. It keeps existing employees happier and more effective when technology they rely on helps them speed up

at critical low-staff periods and training is minimal for rapid onboarding with new staff," explained Pillau.
In order to provide the best possible experience for all parties involved in the industry, people must be considered above convenience and profit.

Although technology offers added convenience for both customers and lodging businesses, at its core, hospitality is about human interaction. In cases where efficiency and speed are expected, technology can help. Automated services are growing among budget and mid-scale hotel brands, where personal interaction isn't typically expected or even desired. However, this consideration must be balanced with employee wellness and customer satisfaction.

CHAPTER TWO

ON THE TECH CAREER TRACK

Software developers are key to the current and ever-evolving face of the hospitality industry. Without innovative application of code, guests wouldn't be able to search for hotels online, make bookings over the internet, check in, or even leave reviews about their experiences online afterward.

Many people who work in the field take advantage of college degree programs such as computer science or software engineering to learn to code and apply their skills to real-world problems. Software developers create and maintain applications like online travel agencies, home-sharing apps, and review and ratings apps such as Yelp. They also create point-of-sale and property management systems for hotel employees to take payments and coordinate guest arrivals and departures.

Aspiring software developers should focus not only on honing coding and math skills but also on paying

Software developers who have knowledge of the hotel industry's standards and practices are well positioned to create new products that improve lodging experiences.

attention to the world and identifying problems that can be solved and processes that may be streamlined by the application of code. Inventive software designers will create the programs that propel the evolution of the hospitality industry throughout the twenty-first century.

COURSES IN CODING

Ambitious interested developers don't necessarily have to enroll in college courses to begin learning to code. Free online resources such as Codecademy, Free Code Camp, and GA Dash offer interactive coding tutorials in a number of different programming languages. EdX is an open-source higher-education program offering free computer science courses in artificial intelligence, cybersecurity, software engineering, and big data offered by MIT and Harvard University. Furthermore, many groups such as Women Who Code offer in-person educational opportunities for young people and underrepresented groups in tech. These learning programs can help students of any age begin to develop facility with code writing and software creation.

To be accepted into a college or university to earn a degree in high-level computer science, students should successfully earn a high school diploma or General Education Development equivalent. However, it is important that aspiring software developers focus not only on honing math and coding skills but also display curiosity in many areas of study. Developing programs is basically a problem-solving process, and software developers can turn their expertise to improving daily experiences for all regardless of their tech proficiency. Software development is a lifelong learning process, as new technologies are continually introduced and improved.

CODING CAREER PATHS

Of course, without the ingenuity of human developers none of this technology would ever have come to exist.

In-room virtual assistant devices allow hotel guests to listen to music, receive travel directions and information about the weather, and even order room service without having to pick up the phone.

Coders who program physical objects, rather than web- or computer-based programs, are known as embedded software developers. This means that they consider the specificities of the hardware—the device they're programming, whether it is a tablet, a TV, a clock, a mirror, or a virtual assistant—in order to ensure their programming works as intended.

Embedded software engineers typically earn undergraduate or graduate-level training in computer science prior to pursuing careers in the field.

RECOVERY THROUGH TECHNOLOGY

Technology can also help rebuild an industry in the wake of a disaster. After suffering the devastation caused by Hurricane Maria in 2017, Puerto Rico turned to technology to help rebuild its once-thriving tourism industry and economy. In a first-of-its-kind effort, Puerto Rico's entire hospitality industry joined forces for the creation of the My Puerto Rico app, made possible by the Puerto Rico Tourism Company. Using the app, visitors could select and communicate with any hotel available on the island. My Puerto Rico's messaging system actually let guests send and receive messages to and from any of the island's hotels, allowing them to ask questions, book services such as babysitting, make reservations, request room service or cleaning, or even coordinate early or late arrival times all through one convenient service.

"In hospitality, we often focus on differentiating hotels from one another," explained Justin Effron, chief executive officer of a partnering company with the app, in an article for *Travel + Leisure* magazine, "but in this case, the Puerto Rico Tourism Company is bringing hotels together to delight all who visit the island."

Puerto Rico's hospitality industry hoped that the added convenience the app provided would prove helpful to tourists and help invigorate the island's economy throughout the post–Hurricane Maria rebuilding process.

Computer engineering, electrical engineering, and even software engineering are common majors that provide a path into the industry. Some embedded software developers work as entrepreneurs, creating their own innovative devices and marketing them to hotels. Others work for large companies like Amazon, helping to create and improve products like the Alexa virtual assistant. Others may seek to work in the hospitality industry directly, using their expertise and training to repair and maintain networks and devices within a hospitality-based business.

Variety is inherent to the field, as an embedded software designer working on, for example, a front-desk automated assistant robot is likely to face a very different workday than another developer working on a smart mirror or automatic room temperature control system. Education is a continual process for embedded software developers: even after obtaining formal education, they must remain ever knowledgeable about emerging technologies and imaginative about their potential applications. Curiosity and a drive to solve problems are necessary qualities in an aspiring embedded software developer.

CYBERSECURITY

Cybersecurity is an important aspect of today's hospitality industry. With so many bookings and transactions taking place online, the threat of hacking, identity theft, or more is a major concern. As a result, cybersecurity experts are in high demand.

Cybersecurity professionals test secure systems in order to identify weaknesses and prevent hackers from accessing vulnerable networks.

Cybersecurity experts have a deep familiarity with computer science and a desire to fix potential weaknesses in tech. "The thing that will make you good at security is that you are great at something else first. For example, become a master of the fundamentals of data networks, be an expert at administering multiple operating systems or be proficient at multiple scripting languages," said Sean Tierney, head of the cyberintelligence team at Infoblox, a privately held information technology automation and security company based in California, in an article for *Forbes* magazine.

In the same article Tierney's colleague Rod Rasmussen, vice president of cybersecurity at Infoblox, recommended network management education through a university to learn security basics but stressed that self-education and continual learning is important for a successful career in cybersafety. "Self-directed learning and experimentation are critical," Tierney agreed, while acknowledging that "college degrees, vendor training and professional certifications are great."

Following the common career path in coding, cybersecurity experts constantly work to remain ahead of new technologies and their applications, anticipating potential points of attack and protecting vulnerable customers from cybercrime. Careers in cybersecurity require a talent for data analysis, a dedication to continual learning, a knack for problem solving, and a desire to protect.

GAINING EXPERIENCE

Hotels rely on skilled tech professionals both to supply and maintain the digital conveniences that endear their accommodations to guests. In a 2016 survey of information technology workers in the hospitality industry conducted for the HITEC Conference Special Report revealed that just over half of the respondents had spent their entire careers working in some aspect of the hospitality field prior to transitioning to IT work. Other respondents previously worked in other industries, such as construction and manufacturing, retail, banking and finance, insurance, and education, before moving into a career in hospitality tech. The report also found overlap between technology-focused employees and the areas of accounting and finance, while other IT employees were also involved in marketing and security.

Such positions do not always require a four-year bachelor's degree or further levels of higher education, but in most cases a degree in computer science or hospitality science is preferred. A good way to gain relevant experience in the hospitality field while gaining qualifications for tech-focused positions is to seek a job in some aspect of hospitality, such as bellhop, valet, or front desk ambassador, while working toward education that will enable IT employment.

Ultimately, the focus of tech in hospitality is to provide for the comfort, convenience, and safety of guests, and a thorough understanding of hotel organization and functionality is necessary for an IT professional to succeed in his or her tasks. Familiarity with the industry is also important for independent tech entrepreneurs who hope to market their software and hardware products to businesses within the field.

The coming chapters will take a look at some of the new and cool technologies that are being developed in hospitality and how computer scientists can find new opportunities in the field.

CHAPTER THREE

CODING MEETS CONCIERGE

In June 2018, Amazon announced a virtual assistant device called Alexa for Hospitality. Geared specifically toward a hotel guest experience, Alexa for Hospitality not only plays music but acts as a sort of in-room digital concierge, providing recommendations for local restaurants and attractions, controlling room temperature and lighting, even allowing guests to order room service or check out of the hotel.

Supported Amazon Echo Dot, Echo, and Echo Plus devices are customized for the particular hotel they service. Installed in guest rooms, Alexa also provides information about the hotels themselves—including pool and fitness center hours, restaurant availability, and other general information—and allows guests to contact hotel services such as the spa, housekeeping, the valet and concierge stations, and the front desk

In 2017, Amazon launched a hotel-focused version of Alexa for Amazon Echo that allows guests to receive restaurant and entertainment recommendations without having to call the front desk.

Alexa for Hospitality is tailored to work with existing hotel technology, such as DigiValet, Intelity, Nuvola, and Volara, to allow guests to book spa appointments and order wine from the comfort of their rooms. When it comes to television entertainment, Alexa can be configured to work with guest room entertainment providers World Cinema and GuestTek to allow guests to operate the TV with voice control. Guests can enjoy music and radio through iHeartRadio and TuneIn, which may be set up to stream playlists coordinated to complement the hotel's brand or the guest's personal taste. Although the feature was unavailable at the product's launch in mid-2018, Amazon is working to allow individual guests to connect to their personal Amazon accounts through Alexa for the length of their stays.

Using a centralized dashboard, hotel employees using the software can easily update information, enable skills, adjust settings, and track usage. The package also allows hotels to measure analytics and track guest engagement, noting trends and altering their services to accommodate customers' patterns. "We will be evaluating guest feedback and adoption to inform how we expand the skills, features, and functionality offered through Alexa in our hotels," said Marriott International's vice president of customer experience innovation, Jennifer Hsieh, in a statement about the system's launch for an article for TechCrunch.

Amazon also works with vacation-rental company RedAwning and boutique hotel properties, such as Thompson Hotels, Joie de Vivre, Destination Hotels, and Alila, to continue testing Alexa for Hospitality.

HUMANS WORKING WITH ROBOTS

In 2016, the robot concierge Connie made its debut in the Hilton McLean Tysons Corner hotel in Virginia. Connie helps guests find attractions, decide where to dine, and locate specific rooms and amenities on the hotel property. Connie's IBM Watson technology allows it to learn as it interacts with guests.

The robot concierge Connie has a humanoid appearance and its actions delight guests checking in at the Hilton McLean Tysons Corner hotel in Virginia.

Standing at about 2 feet (0.6 meters) tall, Connie looks like a humanoid robot from a children's movie. Connie can move its two arms and legs independently to gesture and point in different directions, and its eyes light up with different colors in response to various input. "It's trying to see the person as well as hear the person. It is itself vocalizing and it's using its arm gestures and body language. When it is asked 'where's the elevator?,' it says it's down the hall to the left while pointing down the hall to the left," explained

Rob High, IBM's Watson vice president and chief technology officer in an article for *USA Today*.

But in spite of its abilities and adorable appearance, Connie isn't designed to replace human staffers at the Hilton. In a *USA Today* article, Holthouser said that Connie's introduction was intended to reduce the burden of routine questions and interactions on the human front desk staff, freeing them to check customers in, answer phones, and deal with complex queries from guests that Connie can't handle. For the time being, Connie just answers questions, but in the future Holthouser envisions Connie's skills growing. Perhaps Connie will acquire facial recognition technology to greet loyalty club members personally, be able to search for information during meetings held on the property, or even offer translation services for international guests at the hotel. "I think you're looking at the future," Holthouser said.

Porter 24, a California-based digital concierge service that partners with Marriott, Hilton, and other hotels in the United States, has expanded into more than fifty hotels in New York City. Porter 24's services are provided through screen kiosks in the hotels, rather than face-to-face interaction with a human concierge. The screens allow guests to search for information about local eateries, attractions, and nightlife and are capable of sending detailed directions and information directly to guests' phones. Hotel patrons can also check weather and track flights using the screens and even post to social media if they wish.

DIGITAL CONVENIENCE WITH HUMAN EXPERTISE

In 2017, former luxury concierge Krista Krauss Miller launched an online concierge service named When in Roam in twenty-two large American cities and on the Hawaiian islands Maui and Oahu. This service uses the expertise of real human concierges, who are contracted to create custom travel itineraries based on customers' answers to a special online questionnaire.

When in Roam, Miller explained, is intended to provide the luxury of professional concierge experience and skill to people who are traveling without access to a physical concierge, perhaps travelers staying in an Airbnb or staying with family or friends to save costs. This approach shows the value of concierge service in an increasingly digital world, Miller said in an article for the *New York Times*. "At a time when concierges are more important than ever, hotels are eliminating positions," Miller said.

Her service attempts to combine the benefits of concierge expertise with the convenience of digital accessibility, providing jobs for concierges who need employment and at the same time offering luxury services to travelers who may not be able to afford to stay in traditional high-end hotels.

Colin Perceful, a concierge at the lavish Four Seasons hotel in Seattle, Washington, and also a

(continued on the next page)

(continued from the previous page)

concierge for When in Roam, noted that his digital gig encourages him to stay informed about parts of the city outside of his hotel's downtown base. "There's very little variance among customers in a five-star hotel," Perceful explained, whereas younger travelers staying in Airbnb accommodations or with family or friends force him to reach beyond his typical daily queries in order to provide for their differing tastes. "That's kind of where the concierge profession is trending," he said, noting the hospitality industry's increasing bent toward digital convenience and individualization.

According to research conducted on digital voice assistant owners and released by Google, people are becoming increasingly comfortable interacting with virtual services that mimic human conversation, sometimes even preferring these devices to conversation with real human beings. "The trend matches how people process and access information today, which is increasingly by smartphone," explained Geraldine Guichardo, vice president of Jones Lang Lasalle Americas Hotels Research, in an article for JLL Real Views.

Data gathering capabilities allow digital concierges to store information and learn about guests' preferences as they use the services, leading to more personalized recommendations. Guichardo noted that in addition to offering in-the-moment convenience for travelers, such services can help free up hotel staff to address concerns that require "a human touch," as she put it.

SMART MIRRORS

In 2017, in partnership with cloud-based management platform Keypr, Mirror Image Hospitality created a product called Remi, a smart mirror that serves as a TV and virtual concierge platform. When it's not activated, Remi serves as a simple large mirror in

Smart mirrors allow guests not only to admire their reflections but also to use the devices as a convenient touchscreen service computer.

which guests can see their reflections. At night, the mirror remains dark, rather than interfering with guests' sleep with an electronic light.

A company called Electric Mirror launched the Savvy SmartMirror in both touch- and voice-activated models. In addition to providing information and serving as a digital concierge service, the mirror can track room occupancy and temperature, providing this data to hotel management.

Bjorn Hanson, a clinical professor at the Jonathan M. Tisch Center for Hospitality and Tourism, explained that the appeal of smart mirrors that can perform multiple functions lies in the amount of guest choice the devices provide. "Guests feel entitled to more choices," he said in an article for *Hotel Management* magazine. "The complexity for executives in planning hotel technology is that the guests may change their preferences minute to minute." Smart devices help hotel management better accommodate the quickly shifting whims of guests immediately and conveniently. According to Keypr, hotels using its smart mirror Remi have reported a 20 to 35 percent increase in in-room dining requests thanks to guests ordering room service through the mirror device. This makes sense, say representatives of the services, given that the mirrors' display can be instantly updated with news of sales and photos of daily specials. Smart mirrors drive revenue by tapping into guests' in-the-moment desires, making it easy to place an order.

CHAPTER FOUR

ENHANCING THE STAY

The use of apps and tech tools in the hotel industry has grown enormously since 2010, according to a 2017 *New York Times* article. In the United States, hotel occupancy rates now stand at about 65.5 percent, the highest they've been in nearly thirty-five years. Though the hotel industry was once known to be relatively slow to adopt new technologies, that's changed as guests become more familiar with convenient tech.

Hotels are spending more and more on technology. This commitment is appreciated by twenty-first-century guests, who rely on handheld devices to book rooms, to communicate with staff, to order food, and to leave reviews rating the quality of their experiences.

Marriott hotels' dedicated app, which allows guests to book a room, check in and check out, make requests of hotel staff, and even unlock rooms, has increased customer satisfaction by allowing hotel staff to quickly resolve any problem or issue that may arise at any time of day or night. "You do it all yourself," thirty-year-old Lenette Frye told the *New York Times* of her iPad-enhanced stay at the Four Seasons in Orlando, Florida, noting that she and her husband appreciated the convenience of being able to request services and order food through the device rather than having to leave the room or make a phone call. "I like the ability to do things with the click of a button," said sixty-four-year-old Tina Amber, who prefers to use an in-room iPad to make all her plans while traveling. "If a hotel doesn't have it," she explained, "I'm somewhat put off."

EXPANDING HOSPITALITY SERVICES

Hotel technology also expands the services hotels are capable of offering their customers. Thanks to a recent $28 million renovation and technology update of the Washington Marriott Georgetown hotel in Washington, DC, guests can now use their mobile phones to buy tickets to nearby shows and concerts, make dinner reservations, and have maps sent to their devices at the hotel to make navigating the city easier.

At Chatham Bars Inn, a more than one-hundred-year-old resort located on Cape Cod in Massachusetts, guests can use the hotel's website or mobile app to not only book a room and interact with hotel staff but also to make reservations for things such as a beach cabana or sailboat tour. These digital conveniences help hotels stand out from each other and rival home-sharing apps and online travel agencies, said

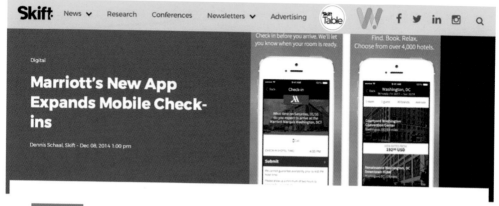

Skift   News ∨   Research   Conferences   Newsletters ∨   Advertising   Skift Table

Check in before you arrive. We'll let you know when your room is ready.

Find. Book. Relax. Choose from over 4,000 hotels.

Digital

Marriott's New App Expands Mobile Check-ins

Dennis Schaal, Skift · Dec 08, 2014 1:00 pm

Skift Take

W hat Marriott is doing on the mobile check-in front will become industry standard over the next few years. In addition, the front desk as a required stop during the check-in process is on the way to becoming extinct.

— *Dennis Schaal*

SHARE

Tweet

Share

in

Marriott redesigned its iOS and Android apps and expanded its mobile check-ins, room-ready alerts and checkout capabilities to some 4,000 properties globally.

These features were previously available at around 1,200 hotels and now the complete roster includes properties at Marriott Hotels, JW Marriott, Renaissance Hotels, Autograph Collection, Marriott Executive Apartments, and AC Hotels by Marriott.

Marriott Rewards members receive a notification a day before arrival to alert them that they can check-in, and then receive room-ready alerts the next day informing them when they can proceed to their rooms. First they must stop by a mobile check-in desk, which provides a streamlined check-in because it doesn't require the presentations of

Mobile applications, such as Marriott's app, as reported in this article, make booking and check-in convenient and easy for travelers accustomed to quickly accessing information on their phones.

Lorraine Sileo, senior vice president for research at Phocuswright, and even form stronger bonds with their customers. "They're trying to improve the guest experience by doing things on the guests' terms instead of the hotel's," explained Gregg Hopkins of Intelity Corporation in regard to hotels' increasing embrace of digital tech. "It drives loyalty and drives repeat business and drives revenue."

PERSONALIZING THE EXPERIENCE

As hospitality tech grows more and more advanced, improving speed and convenience for hotel employees, the focus of improving technology remains fixated on guest comfort. Gretchen Hartley, senior director of global design at Marriott International, said in an article for *Hospitality Technology* magazine:

> **Personalization of the guest experience is the next frontier. We are looking at technology in whatever form as a tool that will help enable this idea. Whether that comes through conversation/voice, Internet of Things, or other guest recognition technology, we are always looking at technology as a way to help further enhance the guest experience.**

Hotel guests respond positively to personalization, and hotels are trying to go beyond simple measures such as temperature control to make customers feel at home in their spaces. According to Ajay Paul of Information Services Group, hotels of the future are going beyond energy-saving room controls and smart mirrors. For example, they are considering installing beds that adjust firmness to guest preferences, automatic coffee makers with built-in WiFi to provide weather and news updates, and even biometric bathroom tiles that are capable of reporting on a guest's health.

In 2018, Hilton announced that its hotels will begin allowing guests to upload their own artwork

Devices integrated into Marriott International, Samsung, and Legrand's internet of things connected hotel room prototype revolutionize the typical hotel guest experience with tech.

and photos to appear on in-room digital displays, further personalizing the hotel experience. Marriott has partnered with Samsung and Legrand to create an Internet of Things Guestroom Innovation Lab that allows guests to access a virtual assistant, smart mirror, and even start the shower at a particular temperature saved in their guest profile through voice or app commands. Meanwhile, Hilton McLean Tysons Corner's Innovation Gallery includes a smart sleep system that eliminates sleep-disturbing noise, a NuCalm branded drug-free relaxation system, and even an automated mixologist that guests can program to make their favorite cocktails in the room.

TRAVELERS WANT TECH

The millennial generation, roughly people ages eighteen to thirty-five in the mid-2010s, has grown to become the largest demographic in the United States, and they wield increasing influence in the field of travel and hospitality.

As more young people travel, technological innovation becomes key in hospitality. Most of them use smartphones and tablets for business and personal reasons while traveling and prefer to stay in a smartphone-enabled hotel that allows check-in and keyless entry via the guest's phone.

According to Yossi Zekri, the president and chief executive officer of Acuant, millennial travelers tend to want their experiences streamlined by technology. Young travelers expect to research destinations, book accommodations, review services, gain access to hotel rooms, and communicate their needs to hotel staff using their phones. There is even an increased desire to choose a hotel that offers personalized service through biometric software such as facial recognition technology.

STREAMING THE COMFORTS OF HOME

On a slightly less exotic note, other hotels are focusing on expanding guest's in-room entertainment streaming options. "Our guests are accustomed to being able to readily access a variety of media options at home on their personal tablets," said Stephen Johnston, managing director and general manager of Boston Harbor Hotel in an article for *Hospitality Technology* magazine. "As their home away from home, we feel strongly that our guestroom technology experience should offer the same level of convenience."

To meet this goal, Boston Harbor Hotel now offers in-room iPads run on the Intelity platform. Concord Hospitality Enterprises makes subscription-based streaming services available on its high-definition TVs, and Samir Lakhany, vice president of Superhost Hospitality, predicts that hotels will stop offering

This tablet from the Aria hotel in Las Vegas allows guests to adjust temperature and lighting, order room service, and enjoy thousands of digital publications at leisure.

cable television content entirely in the near future. Instead, they will simply allow guests to access hotel information and cast entertainment onscreen from their own personal devices.

However, the guest room of the future requires a complex computer network to function. "A guest could be connecting up to five devices at a time in their room," said Jennifer Jones, president of J2 Hospitality Solutions, in an interview with *Hospitality Technology* magazine, and that's in addition to hotel technology such as energy management systems, voice-over internet protocol phone systems, internet protocol television, and wireless key locking systems. To ensure uninterrupted connectivity, hotels are investing in highly secure Ethernet internet connections. Some hotels even use Ethernet to power in-room devices such as TVs and minibars, which helps prevent accidents such as power short outs or guests or employees being electrically shocked.

CONVENIENCE THROUGH APPS

Innovative technology has expanded the traditional way people stay in hotels: check in, spend the night, check out in the morning. Created in 2010, the French app Dayuse allows users to access hotels during the daytime, usually allowing for check-in around 9 a.m. and check-out in the late afternoon. This schedule is particularly convenient for international travelers, who may be suffering from jet lag, or business guests, who might want a place to shower and rest before

Flexible lodging access has revolutionized the way some travelers rest and work, offering convenient options for catching up on sleep and accomplishing remote digitally based tasks in comfort.

meetings, and allows early access to pools, gyms, spas, and meeting spaces at more than four thousand different hotels in twenty-four countries.

ResortPass, a web app launched in 2016, is an online booking platform that allows access to pools, spas, fitness centers, cabanas, and other amenities outside of bedrooms in more than eighty resorts in seven states, including California, Arizona, Florida, and Hawaii. Today the app serves locals on "staycations" who want to use hotel facilities without paying for a room, and home-share and budget travelers who wish to spend the night in more affordable accommodations but still want to take advantage of a higher-end hotel's luxury amenities.

Other apps aim to provide hotel-style room service delivery to guests relaxing on a beach or by a pool. The Florida-based app EazyO uses global positioning satellite technology and a web-based payment platform to allow guests relaxing poolside at, for instance, the Naples Grande Resort, to enjoy delivery from the Fontainebleau Miami Beach resort restaurant. EazyO is described by founder Brett Benza as a "beach butler" enabled by users' iPhones. It can be used not only to order food and drinks but also sunscreen, hats, goggles, beach totes, and more. It even delivers directly to hotel guests' rooms. Hotels who partner with the app are able to offer specials and raise revenue without sacrificing staff time and effort.

CHAPTER FIVE

A CHANGING INDUSTRY

One new technology that is threatening the traditional hotel industry is the online travel agency, also known as OTA. When OTAs, including Expedia, Hotels.com, Hotwire, Travelocity, and Priceline, first rose to prominence around the time of the global economic recession in 2008, they served as a boon to the struggling hotel businesses.

Ten years later, the balance of power in the hospitality industry has shifted: in 2016, OTA lodging bookings in the United States exceeded total hotel website gross bookings for the first time in history. Also, as OTAs have aggregated and gained negotiating power, the commissions they take from hotels have steadily increased. "The reason that many OTAs market rooms better than hotels is because they give consumers everything they're looking for—reviews and recommendations from other travelers, detailed amenity information and realistic photos—all in one

Online travel agencies make booking hotels easy for guests, but they may hurt hospitality businesses' revenue. Many hotels seek to fix this problem by improving their own websites and apps.

place," said Vanessa Vega, global director of hotel distribution and connectivity at Premiere Advisory Group. The one-stop-shopping approach of OTAs is appealing to tech-connected travelers. OTAs also allow for convenient comparison between prices and offerings at various hotels, all on one screen.

The key to encouraging direct booking, modern hoteliers find, lies in increasingly sophisticated, simple-to-navigate website design. Functionality is every bit as important as how a site looks when it comes to securing bookings, Vega emphasized in an article for JLL Real Views. "Today's consumers want to click two or three times and be done with their purchase," Vega said. "If you force people to scroll and look too much, you're making it easier to book via an OTA."

Also, hotels can gain an advantage by offering personalized services for customers who are merely searching for a booking in addition to those they make available during a guest's stay. Travelers looking for good deals, for instance, may wish to easily see price comparison and time-sensitive deals as they browse a hotel's website. Travelers who care more about their experiences, on the other hand, might be more intrigued by amenity packages than pricing. Customer-focused data collection can help equip hotels with the information they need to satisfy various guest preferences. In the end, responsibility falls to hotel website developers to draw eyes, clicks, and ultimately purchases away from OTAs and to drive a shift in direct booking trends.

HOME-SHARING APPS

The enormous popularity of home-sharing apps such as Airbnb, HomeBooking, and Booking.com has disrupted the hospitality industry, inspiring not only technological innovation but also restructuring of the traditional hotel model.

Big-name hotel brands are attempting to break into the home-sharing market. Marriott launched a six-month pilot program with home rental management company Hostmaker to provide more than two hundred carefully selected and vetted homes in London, England, for temporary guest accommodation. Each of the homes, which all come equipped with a full kitchen and laundry facilities, is required to adhere to Marriott hotel standards of safety, design, security, and service and also offer traditional hotel perks such as 24/7 dedicated phone support and in-person check-in.

According to Marriott chief customer experience officer Adam Malamut, this system offers advantages over pure home-sharing options. The Marriott-Hostmaker partnership's resources, on the other hand,

Travel news site Skift reported that traditional hotel businesses seek to corner the home-sharing market by providing the advantages of security, on-call service, and improved amenities for guests.

allow for consistent maintenance of properties carried out by on-the-ground teams. Average prices are also relatively affordable in comparison to luxury Marriott hotel prices.

Choice Hotels International Inc. also announced a major expansion of the vacation rental program it debuted in 2016, adding more than twenty thousand new properties in Orlando, Florida; Myrtle Beach, South Carolina; the Florida Gulf Coast; Lake Tahoe, California; the Outer Banks, North Carolina; Gatlinburg, Tennessee; Maui, Hawaii; and the Colorado Rockies. Like Marriott's program with Hostmaker, Choice's vacation rental properties are managed by local companies that provide on-call support for guests. A month prior to Choice Hotels' expansion, Hyatt Hotels Corporation extended its loyalty program into home-sharing with the home rental company Oasis, which provides more than two thousand homes in twenty locations internationally, expanding Hyatt's presence into Barcelona and Ibiza, Spain; Punta del Este, Uruguay; Rome, Italy; and Trancoso, Brazil.

These developments are a movement across the hospitality industry to adapt to the demand created by home-sharing apps. Millennial and younger travelers, in particular, are attracted to personalized experiences and lifestyle-focused, flexible offerings, noted William Duffey, executive vice president of hotels and hospitality at Jones Lang Lasalle, in an interview. In order for traditional hotel establishments to maintain relevance in the twenty-first century, they must adopt technologically driven business practices that appeal to digitally driven consumers.

NEW WAYS TO PAY

Rapid advances in technology have even affected the way hotels receive payment. When the ability to book lodging online first arose, customers had to pay either with credit cards or bank transfers. Currently, hotel guests have a variety of ways to pay online, such as PayPal, MobilePay, and eWallets.

According to Worldpay's 2017 Global Payments report, 62 percent of all online transactions in 2016 in China, the most populous country in the world, were made using an eWallet. AliPay, China's leading third-party online payment platform, counts over 520 million active monthly users. Online payment is also becoming increasingly popular in Europe, where

Online pay models are becoming increasingly popular with young travelers who are accustomed to using devices to access and pay for services.

Sweden may soon become the modern world's first cash-free society.

Worldpay's 2017 report predicted that eWallets will continue to increase in popularity through 2021, while credit card use will steeply decline. Specifically, credit card use is expected to fall from 29 percent in 2016 to 15 percent by 2021, while eWallet usage is projected to rise dramatically from 18 percent to 46 percent. According to Morten Larsen, head of product marketing for Booking.com, in an article for Click by Booking.com, as many as one in five potential customers will back out of completing a reservation if his or her payment method of choice is not offered. Offering multiple methods of online payment is key to attract customers in the contemporary digital world.

BLOCKCHAIN AND BUSINESS

For hotel businesses affected by the typical 15 to 20 percent commissions charged by large OTAs, blockchain platforms could be the key to reclaiming bookings and even reducing guest prices. A blockchain is essentially a digital ledger of records linked using cryptography, which is resistant to alteration. By their nature, blockchains are considered very secure.

The startup Travala uses the blockchain platform to support a decentralized, commission-free

(continued on the next page)

(continued from the previous page)

hotel-booking platform, claiming that its model could save customers up to 45 percent on traditional booking fees. LockTrip, a similar company, rolled out its services in late 2018. These booking platforms could also allow potential hotel guests to pay with cryptocurrency like Bitcoin, eliminating traditional payment processing fees.

However, blockchain's future in the hotel industry remains to be seen. Its use in the hospitality industry is limited, but its adoption may have the potential to disrupt traditional business practices in the field.

DIGITAL SECURITY

Of course, security is a major concern when it comes to online payments and booking. The use of bots (programs designed to interact with computer systems and users) to steal and abuse people's credentials is a risk for all internet-driven businesses. Akamai Technology's State of the Internet/Security Summer 2018 report showed that the hospitality industry faces particular danger in this regard, suffering significantly more identity theft than other industries studied. In an analysis of 112 billion bot requests and 3.9 billion malicious log-in attempts across airline, cruise, and hotel websites, Akamai researchers found that almost 40 percent of the traffic across hotel and travel sites is classified as "impersonators of known browsers," in attempts at fraud. Geographic analysis showed that Russia, China, and Indonesia were the largest sources of bot-driven fraud attempts during the period observed by the study.

This bot-assisted "attack traffic" was so common in Russia and China, in particular, that those two countries combined generated three times more attack attempts than the total amount of attack traffic generated in the United States. "These countries have historically been large centers for cyberattacks, but the attractiveness of the hospitality industry appears to have made it a significant target for hackers to carry out bot-driven fraud," explained senior security advocate Martin McKeay in the 2018 Akamai State of the Internet/Security Report.

The most common method of attacking hospitality industry organizations is DDoS, or distributed denial of service attacks, which paralyze computer networks by flooding them with an enormous volume of data sent from many individual computers at the same time, overwhelming the online service and making it unavailable. These attacks often rely on a coordinated group of bot programs infected with malware to carry out hacker commands.

Other attacks are carried out by human volunteers who organize their efforts through group chats online. Another type of attack overwhelms the target's domain name system server by sending bursts of data instead of a sustained attack, making this kind of attack more difficult to predict and prevent. "These attacks should serve as a not-so-gentle reminder that the security community can never grow complacent," McKeay warned in the Akamai Report. Unfortunately, the problem is only likely to grow more challenging as time goes on and digital criminals become more sophisticated. In 2018, Akamai recorded a 16 percent increase in DDoS attacks on the hospitality industry since 2017.

HOTELS MEET HOSTELS

Technology also allows for a middle ground between tech-filled hotels and affordable hostels. PodShare, a unique "co-living" space, with five locations around

New, nontraditional hostels, such as PodShare, with its motto of "access, not ownership," promote the embrace of shared accommodations for affordable prices.

Los Angeles, is made up of a single large space filled with individual beds that convert into desks during the day. Combining sleeping and working space in a single inexpensive location, PodShare serves as a sort of combination hostel and office. Each of these "pods" is equipped with a laptop and mobile phone charging station and individual TV with streaming services. PodShare spaces offer affordable rates for young travelers who don't mind sharing living and coworking space with others, but the appeal of the unconventional accommodation lies not only in the social nature of the space but in its plugged-in embrace of digital technology.

In 2016, founder Elvina Beck described the company as "membership-based housing across multiple locations," in an article for Business Insider, explaining that guests can access any of the five locations throughout the city with a keypad code for the duration of their stays.

PodShare mainly serves a young demographic of "travelers, transitioners, and temps," that is— tourists visiting the Los Angeles area, people who need an affordable place to stay while locating long-term living quarters in the city, and employees working temporary time-limited jobs, such as film production assistants, who need somewhere to stay for the duration of their gigs. "I started it to cure my own loneliness, so I never had a night without friends," said Beck in an interview with Motherboard. Today, she lives in a pod full-time with a rotating assortment of temporary roommates.

TECHNOLOGY AND INCREASING COMPETITION

Not all online travel agencies are market-dominating giants, however, and small OTAs use creativity and convenience to stay competitive. As a mobile-only app that analyzes billions of flights to help users find the best travel deals, Hopper finds it difficult to compete with larger OTAs. To attract travelers, Hopper focuses on the benefits of its mobile-only platform, offering features that can't be replicated on a desktop computer. Hopper acquires most of its customers through social media, giving users the opportunity to book immediately for the current lowest price or wait and receive notification from the app when prices drop even lower.

Another mobile-only app, HotelTonight, similarly takes advantage of this platform. "Being mobile-first has enabled a level of focus that means we can outcompete the legacy OTAs in booking speed and simplicity, which keeps our bookers coming back," explained HotelTonight CEO Sam Shank.

MyFlightSearch, a small price comparison and booking app, attracts repeat travelers by offering superior customer service to large OTAs, tracking clients' searches and preferences, and working personally to resolve any issues that may arise.

"The legacy OTAs have deeper pockets when it comes to marketing, to be sure, but they've forgotten how to innovate," said HotelTonight's Shank. Ultimately, technological innovation and consideration of travelers' needs serves to shape all aspects of the hospitality industry, from the smallest to the largest businesses.

CHAPTER SIX

THE NEW LOOK OF HOSPITALITY

Technology has profoundly affected marketing and sales strategies for the hospitality industry. Word of mouth recommendations and positive reviews have always been a boon for hotels around the globe, but the immediacy of the internet makes

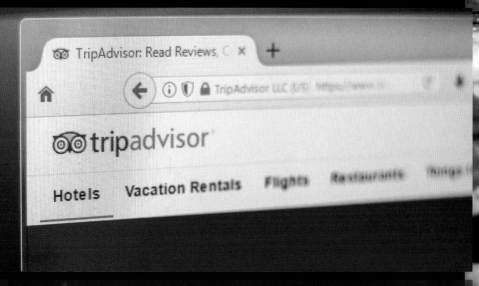

Online customer reviews are vitally important to the success of hospitality businesses, as positive guest ratings influence future travelers' decisions about where to stay.

it easier than ever for a satisfied (or angry!) guest to share stories and opinions about his or her experience with others online. Receiving good reviews on business websites and local-search services such as Yelp are very important to hotels in the twenty-first century. Furthermore, social media has created new avenues for advertising hospitality businesses' spaces and services.

THE POWER OF INSTAGRAM

According to *Travel + Leisure* magazine's Dobrina Zhekova, "the new gold standard for hotels is how great it's going to look on Instagram." According to Instagram data, seven of the most geo-tagged hotels in the world in 2017 are located in Las Vegas, Nevada, including the Bellagio, the Venetian, MGM Grand, The Cosmopolitan, Wynn, Caesar's Palace, and Paris Las Vegas Hotel & Casino. Atlantis The Palm in Dubai, United Arab Emirates, also made the list, as did the Fontainebleau Miami Beach in Florida and Ushuaïa Ibiza Beach Hotel in Spain.

Perhaps the most Instagram-famous hotel in the world is the Marina Bay Sands Singapore, which features an enormous infinity pool on its rooftop, overlooking the Singapore city skyline from fifty-seven floors up. The iconic building, which also contains a SkyPark, live theater shows, shopping centers, multiple restaurants, and a museum, made appearances in the box-office record-breaking movie *Crazy Rich Asians*.

Not all hotels that benefit from Instagram exposure are expensive luxury experiences, however. In 2018,

Buzzfeed compiled a list of the most "Instagramable" hostels around the world, all of which charge under $150 (US dollars) per night. In addition to the 7 Fells Hostel in Akaslompolo, Finland, for its stunning views of the Northern Lights; Ccasa Hostel in Nha Trang, Vietnam, for its innovative architecture and indoor hammocks; and infinity pool–equipped 99 Surf Lodge, in Popoyo, Nicaragua, Buzzfeed's affordable picturesque finds also included the individually themed rooms of the Die Wohngemeinschaft hostel in Cologne, Germany, where guests can sleep in a spaceship bed, and the Santos Express Train Lodge of

Modern hostels, such as Die Wohngemeinschaft in Cologne, Germany, use the attraction of specially themed, affordable rooms to entice potential guests.

Mossel Bay, South Africa, that is actually built inside an abandoned train!

Web design and marketing is another profoundly important aspect of the hospitality industry, serving to attract customers and solidify hotels' brands. As revealed by the HITEC 2016 Special Report, a number of information technology workers in the hotel industry also oversee aspects of marketing, turning their talents toward social media marketing and website creation and maintenance.

LUXURY ACCOMMODATIONS IN A GALAXY FAR, FAR AWAY

A new American hotel is using previously unimagined technology to transport guests to space ... or the next best thing. Walt Disney World Resort will connect seamlessly to the park's new Star Wars: Galaxy's Edge attraction. Every room of the resort is reported to offer a window into what appears to be outer space.

Upon arriving, guests are dressed in universe-appropriate costuming and greeted as if they are citizens of the Star Wars galaxy, taking part in an interactive story featuring brand-new in-universe characters operating a starship voyaging through the galaxy.

Travelers who wish to experience the thrill of a space adventure without actually leaving Earth are eager for the fun to begin. "It's unlike anything that exists today," said Bob Chapek, chairman of Walt Disney Parks & Resorts, while announcing the hotel at the D23 Expo fan event at Disneyland. "It is 100 percent immersive, and the story will touch every single minute of your day, and it will culminate in a unique journey for every person who visits."

HITEC AND INDUSTRY EDUCATION

The Hospitality Industry Technology Exposition and Conference, abbreviated as HITEC, is the largest international hospitality technology exposition and conference. HITEC is produced by the Hospitality Financial and Technology Professionals association, which held the first international hospitality conference devoted to industry technology in 1972. Back then, the cutting-edge technology making waves in the hotel industry included front office property management systems, electronic cash registers, and point-of-sale systems. Today, the focus rests on twenty-first century developments such as customer relationship management software, in-room internet, and handheld computers.

The 2016 HITEC event held in New Orleans, Louisiana, was one of the most popular conferences in the organization's history, hosting more than six thousand hospitality professionals from sixty-five different countries. The 867 exhibit booths included in the 2016 conference showcased various tech related to the internet of things, robotics, mobility, and payment security. It was such a success that the organization decided to expand. In 2017, the

(continued on the next page)

(continued from the previous page)

Hospitality Financial and Technology Professionals association not only sponsored its annual HITEC event in the United States but also added two brand-new events in Europe and the Middle East in order to address growing demand for high-tech adoption in the industry.

The 2018 annual American HITEC event was the largest in the association's history, with more than 6,650 attendees and nearly four hundred vendors. The closing keynote address was given by former White House chief intelligence officer and cybersecurity expert Theresa Payton, emphasizing the hospitality industry's continually increasing focus on protecting guest data from cybercriminals.

A HIGH-TECH FUTURE

It's clear that technology is woven throughout every aspect of the hospitality industry for both guests and employees. Computer science drives the experience of convenience and comfort for customers and allows workers to do their jobs with a minimum of hassle. Creative coders focused on software, devices, and security have brought hospitality into the twenty-first century and will continue to push the boundaries of travel and lodging in the future. Curiosity, customer service, and a deep appreciation of the power of computers can propel anyone into a successful career in the field of hospitality.

Alexa A virtual assistant developed and marketed by Amazon.

app Short for "application," a specialized program downloaded to a user's mobile device.

automation Technology that can function independently without the continual oversight of a human operator.

biometrics The measurement and analysis of unique physical or behavioral characteristics (such as fingerprint or voice patterns) as a means of verifying personal identity.

blockchain A digital record in which transactions made in bitcoin or another cryptocurrency are recorded chronologically and publicly.

bot An automated program that runs over the internet.

concierge A hotel employee whose job is to assist guests by arranging tours, making theater and restaurant reservations, and so on.

DDoS Short for "distributed denial of service attacks," which paralyze computer networks by flooding them with an enormous volume of data sent from many individual computers at the same time.

Ethernet A system for connecting a number of computer systems to form a local area network via a wired connection.

e-wallet A type of electronic card, which is used for transactions made online through a computer or a smartphone.

home-sharing An arrangement by which two or more unrelated people share a dwelling within which each retains a private space. For example, an owner may rent his or her living space to a guest while he or she is traveling elsewhere.

hostel An establishment that provides inexpensive food and lodging for students, workers, or travelers.

internet of things The network of physical objects that are embedded with computers allowing them to connect to the internet and one another.

millennial A member of the generation born between the years 1981 and 1996.

OTA Short for "online travel agency," a website that helps travelers locate and book accommodations.

POS system Short for "point of sale," a combination of hardware and software built to centralize business operations.

self-service kiosk A booth with a computer that dispenses information or makes sales via a touchscreen.

smart mirror A device that not only allows its user to observe his or her reflection but also accesses apps for various other purposes such as playing music, looking up information, and so on.

social media Websites and other online means of communication that are used by large groups of people to share information and to develop social and professional contacts.

streaming service A usually subscription-based program that allows video or audio content sent in compressed form over the internet to be played immediately, allowing the user to watch or listen without downloading.

American Hotel & Lodging Educational Foundation
1250 Eye Street NW, Suite 1100
Washington, DC 20005-3931
(202) 289-3180
Website: https://www.ahlef.org
Facebook and Twitter: @AHLEFoundation
Instagram: @ahlefoundation
The American Hotel & Lodging Educational Foundation
is a nonprofit affiliate of the American Hotel &
Lodging Association (AHLA) focused on providing
scholarships to a small group of promising
hospitality students.

British Columbia Hotel Association
200 - 948 Howe Street
Vancouver, BC V6Z 1N9
(604) 681-7164
Website: http://bchotelassociation.com
The British Columbia Hotel Association is an advocate
for the interests of the hotel industry throughout
British Columbia.

Hotel Association of Canada
1206-130 Albert Street
Ottawa, ON K1P-5G4
(613) 237-7149
Website: http://www.hotelassociation.ca
Twitter: @hotelassoc
The Hotel Association of Canada is the leading voice
of the Canadian Hotel & Lodging industry, delivering

advocacy for sustainability solutions for the hotel industry across Canada.

Hotel Technology Next Generation

650 E. Algonquin Road, Suite 207
Schaumburg, IL 60173
(847) 303-5560
Website: https://www.htng.org
Facebook: @HTNG
Twitter: @htng
Hotel Technology Next Generation is the global nonprofit trade association that fosters development of next-generation solutions.

International Ecotourism Society

PO Box 96503 #34145
Washington, DC 20090-6503
(202) 506-5033
Website: http://www.ecotourism.org
Facebook: @ecotravelpage
Twitter: @ecotravel
Instagram: @ties_ecotourism
The International Ecotourism Society is a nonprofit association committed to promoting responsible tourism practices that benefit conservation and communities.

International Hotel and Restaurant Association

5 Avenue Theodore Flournoy
1207 Geneva
+4122-5948145
Website: http://www.ih-ra.org

The International Hotel and Restaurant Association is
a nonprofit organization recognized by the United
Nations for promoting and defending the interests
of the hotel and restaurant industry worldwide.

U.S. Travel Association
1100 New York Avenue NW, Suite 450
Washington, DC 2000
(202) 408-8422
Website: https://www.ustravel.org
Facebook: @U.S.TravelAssociation
Twitter: @USTravel
Instagram: @ustravel_association
The U.S. Travel Association is a national nonprofit
organization representing all components of the
travel industry.

Althoff, Corey. *The Self-Taught Programmer: The Definitive Guide to Programming Professionally*. San Francisco, CA: Triangle Connection LLC, 2017.

Boella, M. J. *Human Resource Management in the Hotel and Catering Industry*. New York, NY: Routledge, 2018.

Brookshear, Glenn, and Dennis Brylow. *Computer Science: An Overview* (What's New in Computer Science). 13th ed. London, England: Pearson, 2018.

Hare, Kevin, and Pindar Arman. *Computer Science Principles: The Foundational Concepts of Computer Science—For AP Computer Science Principles*. Atlanta, GA: Yellow Dart Publishing, 2018.

Hayes, David, and Jack Ninemeier. *Human Resources Management in the Hospitality Industry*. Hoboken, NJ: John Wiley & Sons, Inc., 2016.

Hayes, David, et al. *Hotel Operations Management*. London, England: Pearson, 2016.

Johnson, Brandon, and Katherine Foley Roden. *Hospitality from the Heart: Engage Your Employees, Deliver Extraordinary Service, and Create Loyal Guests*. Edina, MN: Beaver's Pond Press, 2013.

Kenny, Conor. *Dancing at the Fountain: In Conversation with World-Leading Hoteliers*. Cork, Ireland: Oak Tree Press, 2016.

Legrand, Willy, et al. *Sustainability in the Hospitality Industry: Principles of Sustainable Operations*. New York, NY: Routledge, 2017.

McGuire, Kelly, and Jeannette Ho. *Hotel Pricing in a Social World: Driving Value in the Digital Economy*. Hoboken, NJ: John Wiley & Sons, Inc., 2016.

Solomon, Micah, and Herve Humler. *The Heart of Hospitality: Great Hotel and Restaurant Leaders Share Their Secrets*. New York, NY: SelectBooks, Inc., 2016.

Walker, John. *Introduction to Hospitality*. London, England: Pearson, 2016.

Walker, John, and Jack Miller. *Supervision in the Hospitality Industry*. Hoboken, NJ: John Wiley & Sons, Inc., 2017.

Akamai Press Release. "Akamai State of the Internet/ Security Summer 2018: Web Attack Report Shows Hospitality Industry Under Siege From Botnets." Akamai, June 26, 2018. https://www.akamai .com/us/en/about/news/press/2018-press /akamai-releases-summer-2018-state-of-the -internet-security-report.jsp.

Biesiada, Jamie. "In Land of the Giants, Smaller OTAs Find Ways to Grab Customers." Travel Weekly, June 6, 2018. https://www.travelweekly .com/Travel-News/Travel-Technology /Smaller-OTAs-find-ways-to-grab-customers.

Bradford, Laurence. "How to Start a Lucrative Career in Cybersecurity." *Forbes*, February 27, 2017. https://www.forbes.com/sites /laurencebradford/2017/02/27/how-to-start-a -lucrative-career-in-cybersecurity/#2e8b2dc01066.

Calderon, Arielle. "13 Instagramable Hostels from Around the World That Are Cheap AF." Buzzfeed, July 28, 2018. https://www.buzzfeed.com /ariellecalderon/hostels-from-around-the-world.

Edleson, Harriet. "Putting the Front Desk in the Hotel Guest's Pocket." *New York Times*, April 24, 2017. https://www.nytimes.com/2017/04/24/business /putting-the-front-desk-in-the-hotel-guests-pocket .html.

Escobar, Michal Christine. "The Guestroom of the Future: Hyper-Personalized, Hyper-Connected." *Hospitality Technology*, February 8, 2018. https:// hospitalitytech.com/guestroom-future-hyper -personalized-hyper-connected.

Fickley-Baker, Jennifer. "Star Wars-Inspired Resort Planned for Walt Disney World Resort Promises to be 'Unlike Anything That Exists Today.'" Disney Parks Blog, February 11, 2018. https://disneyparks.disney.go.com/blog/2018/02/d23j-update-star-wars-hotel.

Fox, Jena Tesse. "Smart Mirrors Are Helping Redefine the Hotel Guest Experience." *Hotel Management*, May 24, 2018. https://www.hotelmanagement.net/tech/how-smart-mirrors-are-changing-way-guests-interact-hotel-rooms.

Glusac, Elaine. "3 New Services That Bring Hotel Amenities to Travelers Not in Hotels." *New York Times*, June 25, 2018. https://www.nytimes.com/2018/06/25/travel/resortpass-easyo-dayuse-app.html.

Holmes, Natalie. "Computer Says Yes: Why Hotels Are Employing Digital Concierges." JLL Real Views, July 27, 2018. https://www.jllrealviews.com/industries/hospitality/ok-computer-hotels-employing-digital-concierges.

Holmes, Natalie. "How Hotel Brands Are Cracking the Home Rental Market." JLL Real Views, May 24, 2018. https://www.jllrealviews.com/industries/hotels/hotel-brands-cracking-home-rental-market.

JLL Staff Reporter. "Hotels Step Up Their Online Game to Encourage Direct Bookings." JLL Real Views, January 15, 2018. https://www.jllrealviews.com/industries/hotels-step-up-their-online-game-to-encourage-direct-bookings.

Killion, Christine. "Hoteliers Look to Streamline and Integrate Technologies at HITEC." Lodging, June 22,

2018. http://lodgingmagazine.com/hoteliers-look
-connect-integrate-tech-solutions-hitec-2018.

Larsen, Morten. "Evolution of Online Payments." Click,
July 2, 2018. https://click.booking.com
/opinion/2018/07/02
/evolution-of-online-payments.

Perez, Sarah. "Amazon Launches an Alexa System
for Hotels." TechCrunch, June 19, 2018. https://
techcrunch.com/2018/06/19
/amazon-launches-an-alexa-system-for-hotels.

Pillau, Uli. "The One Thing Every Hotel Should Consider
When Purchasing Hotel Technology." Hospitality.net,
June 13, 2018. https://www.hospitalitynet.org
/opinion/4088840.html.

Poling, Monica. "More Details Emerge About Disney's
Star Wars Hotel." Travel Pulse, July 7, 2018.
https://www.travelpulse.com/news
/hotels-and-resorts/more-details-emerge-about
-disney-s-star-wars-hotel.html.

Reuters. "U.S. Hotels Arm Staff with Panic Buttons,
After Years of Resistance." *New York Times*,
September 6, 2018. https://www.nytimes.com
/reuters/2018/09/06/us/06reuters-usa-hotels
-abuse.html.

Rizzo, Cailey. "A Year After Hurricane Maria, Puerto
Rico Is Investing in New Technology to Bring Back
Tourists." *Travel + Leisure*, August 31, 2018.
https://www.travelandleisure.com/travel-news
/my-puerto-rico-app-hotels.

Seely, Mike. "The Great Concierge Debate: Digital or
Personal?" *New York Times*, October 20, 2017.
https://www.nytimes.com/2017/10/20/travel

/digital-vs-personal-concierges.html.

Short, Taylor. "Guest Preferences for Technology Use in Hotels IndustryView | 2015." Software Advice, Inc., February 5, 2015. https://www.softwareadvice.com/hotel-management/industryview/technology-use-report-2015.

Stokes, Natasha. "Modern Hospitality: Striking the Right Balance Between High-Tech and Human." JLL Real Views, October 5, 2017. https://www.jllrealviews.com/industries/hospitality/modern-hospitality-striking-the-right-balance-between-high-tech-and-human.

Tenorio, Alejandra. "Brett Benza Dishes on Eazy O, the New Beachside Delivery App Taking Over Miami." Haute Living, April 3, 2018. https://hauteliving.com/2018/04/brett-benza-dishes-eazy-o-beachside-delivery-app/653847.

Ting, Deanna. "Marriott Experiments with Homesharing." Skift, April 23, 2018. https://skift.com/2018/04/23/marriott-experiments-with-homesharing.

Tozzi, Christopher. "How Blockchains Are Changing the Hotel Industry." Nasdaq.com, May 15, 2018. https://www.nasdaq.com/article/how-blockchains-are-changing-the-hotel-industry-cm963808.

Trejos, Nancy. "Introducing Connie, Hilton's new robot concierge." *USA Today*, March 9, 2016. https://www.usatoday.com/story/travel/roadwarriorvoices/2016/03/09/introducing-connie-hiltons-new-robot-concierge/81525924.

United States Bureau of Labor Statistics *Occupational Outlook Handbook*. "Lodging Managers." United

States Department of Labor, April 13, 2018. https://www.bls.gov/ooh/management/lodging -managers.htm#tab-4.

United States Bureau of Labor Statistics *Occupational Outlook Handbook*. "Occupational Employment and Wages, May 2017 43-4081 Hotel, Motel, and Resort Desk Clerks." United States Department of Labor, March 31, 2018. https://www.bls.gov/oes /current/oes434081.htm#ind.

Venega, Tanya. "Today's Hospitality IT Professional." HITEC 2016 Special Report, June 2016. http:// www.mydigitalpublication.com.

Zekri, Yossi. "Authenticity and Technology—the Millennial Essentials." Boutique Hotel News, February 1, 2016. https://www.boutiquehotelnews .com/home/features/2016/2/1 /authenticity-and-technology-the-millennial -essentials.

Zhekova, Dobrina. "These Are the Most Popular Hotels on Instagram in 2017." *Travel + Leisure*, November 29, 2017. https://www.travelandleisure.com /hotels-resorts/most-instagrammed-hotels.

INDEX

ABOUT THE AUTHOR

Jennifer Culp is a medical editor and author of numerous nonfiction science and technology books for young adults.

PHOTO CREDITS